1/4/2010

Beloved Whitney,

Be steadfast, immovable, always abounding in the work of the Lord. (1 Corin 15:58)

Be blessed.

Love,

Ms. Jo Anne

# On Solid Ground

## Inspirational Poetry for All Occasions

### Jo Anne Meekins

"Trust in the Lord with all thine heart; and lean not unto thine own understanding. In all thy ways acknowledge him, and he shall direct thy paths." (Proverbs 3:5-6)

authorHOUSE®

*AuthorHouse*™
*1663 Liberty Drive, Suite 200*
*Bloomington, IN 47403*
*www.authorhouse.com*
*Phone: 1-800-839-8640*

*First published by AuthorHouse 4/9/2008*

*ISBN: 978-1-4343-7273-4 (sc)*

*Library of Congress Control Number: 2008903473*

*Printed in the United States of America*
*Bloomington, Indiana*

*This book is printed on acid-free paper.*

# Dedication

This book is dedicated to the following people who have given me life, nurtured, and supported me:

To my mother, **Phyllis Bynum**, thank you for doing the best you knew how then and for the love you demonstrate to me now. I love and appreciate you.

To my late grandparents, **James** and **Bernice Bynum**, who are forever alive in my heart of memories, thank you for your loving hearts, open house, and generous provisions. You were my rock, my hope, and the instruments that pointed me to my faith and hope in God.

To my late father, **William Meekins**, thank you for loving my mother, for contributing to my birth, and for naming me.

To my daughter **Tina**, your spirit is always and forever alive in my consciousness; I love and experience you through the heart of God.

# Acknowledgements

To **God** be the glory, great things He has done!

My brothers in Christ, **Ouemonde** and **Remonde Brangman**, who discipled me in college and introduced me to my first home church. I am eternally grateful.

My home church families of **First Church of God**, Far Rockaway, NY (1981-1995); **St. Paul Community Baptist Church**, Brooklyn, NY (1995-2005); and **Crossroads Tabernacle**, Bronx, NY (2005-Present). You are my places of preparation and spiritual foundation.

The faculty and classmates of **Inner Visions Institute for Spiritual Development**, Silver Spring, MD (8/2006-3/2007); thank you for teaching me about completing incomplete cycles of action and Living Vision Action Plans.

My **Sister-Friends**: Jossie, Cassandra, Taaliba, Joy, Gretchen, Flora, Jacqueline, Judy, and Lisa; my **Sister-Daughters**: Susan and Josette; my **Brother-Friends**: Kevin, Bill, LaMont, Cortez, Eustace, and Mike; I treasure you all and love you dearly.

# Contents

## Section One:  WORDS OF ENCOURAGEMENT

## Section Two:  WORDS OF CHALLENGE

## Section Three: WORDS OF RELATIONSHIP

## Section Four: WORDS OF CELEBRATION

## Section Five:  WORDS OF COMFORT

## Section Six: WORDS OF TESTIMONY

## Section Seven: ETHNOCENTRIC EXPRESSIONS

# Section One (1)

## Words Of Encouragement

The poems in Section One include 1) HOPE; 2) Look Up
When You're Down; 3) When; 4) A Faithful Companion; 5) Be
Encouraged; 6) The Victory Is Ours; 7) Choices; 8) Thought Power.

This section serves to encourage individuals who may experience
feelings of hopelessness, depression, loneliness, defeat, indecision, or
low self-esteem.

# Hope

**H** - Having faith and helping others to endure,
    believe, and pray.

**O** - Omnipotent, Omniscient, Omnipresent;
    Optimistically, overcoming all obstacles
    everyday, in every season of every
    second, and every minute of every hour.

**P** - Persevering, pressing toward the prize;
    Being fully present and possessing power.

**E** - Embracing yourself, your future, and your destiny.
    Expectantly enlightened now unto eternity.

Completely surrendered to the HOPE in Christ
helps you live life successfully!

(Romans 15:13) *"Now the God of hope fill you with all joy and peace
in believing, that ye may abound in hope, through the power of the Holy
Spirit."*

# Look Up When You're Down

Do you ever have days when your spirit is low?
When you ask yourself why, but you don't even know?
When you're not quite yourself, lost your get up and go?

Do you mope and find fault with this world and mankind?
Do you yield to your mood and feel hopeless inside?
Do you look to your future and would rather die?

If you do, look to God, who faithful and true.
God will love you and keep you and free your mind too.
With God on your side, there is nothing you can't do.

Through God's divine power, you can survive these last days;
Just ask God to help you and believe as you pray.
Hold fast to God's promises, He will make a way.


(Psalms 121:1-2) *"I lift up mine eyes unto the hills, whence cometh my help. My help cometh from the Lord, which made heaven and earth."*

# When

When you're feeling lost and lonely,
turn to Jesus Christ and say:
"Help me Lord, please help me
not to feel this way.

Let me feel your presence
as you fill this void inside,
Become my Lord and Savior,
my Protector and my Guide."

When emotions overwhelm you
and pools of tears stream down your face,
Ask God to be your comfort
with His mercy and His grace.

God will hear you if you seek Him
with a heart that is sincere;
He will walk you through your struggles
and deliver you from your fears.

When painful memories from your past
shadow the good that you try to do,
Confess and release them to the Lord,
He can heal the hurt in you.

Accept his Holy Spirit,
He can change your life around
and make you a better person
with a mind that is clear and sound.

When you know God, you will love Him
and be loved beyond compare.
You'll no longer choose to settle
once you've experienced
God's priceless care.

God promises to never leave you
and to supply your every need.
He can help you resolve all your problems
and give you the power to succeed.

(Romans 10:9) *"That if thou confess with thy mouth the Lord Jesus, and shalt believe in thine heart that God hath raised him from the dead, thou shalt be saved."*

# A Faithful Companion

Outwardly,
You show a carefree spirit
throughout your problems
and your plights;

But inwardly,
When you're overwhelmed and crying,
do you know that Jesus is available
morning, noon, and night?

No matter what you're going through,
you don't have to handle it alone;
Christ can intercede for you
to our heavenly Father on the throne.

God knows everything about you
and will receive you as you are.
If you confess and yield your fears to Him,
He will heal your inner scars.

God can fill the void you're feeling
and ease the pain within your heart.
When you accept His Holy Spirit,
He will never fail you nor depart.

Jesus Christ, the blessed Savior,
will be your brother and parent too.
You'll never find a more faithful companion,
who will forever stand by you.

You don't have to live life frightened,
just put your trust in God above.
God will give you strength to persevere
through His presence and His love.

(Hebrews 4:16) *"Let us therefore come boldly unto the throne of grace,
that we may obtain mercy, and find grace to help in time of need."*

# Be Encouraged

Be strengthened through your struggles
And allow grace to ease the pain.
Don't despair in situations,
Your perseverance is not in vain.

The good work that God's begun in you
Will be completed unto the end.
Be encouraged throughout the journey
And let Christ become your closest friend.

Study God's word and stand on His promises,
They are there for you to claim.
God loves you so completely
And He knows your need and name.

Lean not to your own understanding,
Receive peace and comfort,
And let the Holy Spirit guide.
Call on Jesus and experience the power
That has been tested and been tried.

(Psalms 42:5) *"Why art thou cast down, O my soul? and why art thou disquieted in me? hope in God: for I shall yet praise him for the help of his countenance."*

# The Victory Is Ours

Satan tries to treat us like we're his toys;
He attacks us daily to try and steal our joy.
But, it won't work unless we allow it to
Because the God we serve is faithful and true.

If we resist the devil and don't give in,
Through Christ, our Savior, we can always win.
When we're obedient to God and boldly speak our faith,
We can rebuke old Satan to keep him in his place.

We will never be tempted beyond what we can bear
When we yield to God's will and stay under His care.
When tempted or angry, and want to sin, punch, or shout,
Remember that God will always provide a way out.

(I Corinthians 10:13) *"There hath no temptation taken you but such as is common to man: but God is faithful, who will not suffer you to be tempted above that ye are able; but will with the temptation also make a way to escape, that ye may be able to bear it."*

# Choices

You're exposed to a world filled with strife and turmoil.
Satan prowls around in waiting to destroy.
Disguising all his traps and dangers to entice you,
Using peer-pressure, drugs, and sex as youthful ploys.

Satan's a master at distorting truth and reason;
He can make you think his ways are fun, you see.
And when you are persuaded to join with him,
You will find yourself in deep, dark misery.

Then you will see he's not your friend,
he only wants to do you in,
confuse your mind, and leave you
lost, and alone in sin.

But take heart and learn of God, who truly loves you.
He will lift you up and give you peace of mind.
Cast your troubles onto God, He will relieve you
And you'll be blessed beyond compare in your lifetime.

Believe in God, who created your innermost being.
Give God the praise because you are wonderfully made.
God has searched you and He knows you so completely,
Before your birth, throughout your life, in every way.

God's great love surpasses human understanding;
He designed salvation's plan to set us free.
Since we all were born into this world as sinners,
God sent Christ to die as our redemption fee.

(I Peter 5:6-7) *"Humble yourselves therefore under the mighty hand of
God, that he may exalt you in due time: Casting all your care upon him;
for he careth for you."*

# Thought Power

The thoughts you think are critical
to who you will become,
Positive or negative conditioning
is the determining key.

Take captive every thought
and filter it through your mind,
Weed out the negative
to achieve your positive destiny.

Ideally, learning should begin
while in the mother's womb:
Reading, music, and talking
all should play a part.

Daily affirmations, heritage,
and unconditional love
Are seeds of greatness
to be planted in the heart.

The power of the mind
can help you accomplish any goals,
Just put your plan in action
and persistently follow through.

If you believe you can achieve it
and that you deserve the best,
Then there is nothing
that you can not successfully do.

Unfortunately, there are some of us
put down throughout their lives,
who think they won't amount to anything.

But, opportunities arise each day,
a chance to turn the tide,
A renewing for the lost, long-suffering.

Thus, meditate on things of good report,
praiseworthy, just, and pure.
Perceive yourself the way you were created to be.

Know that you are a divine creation
with a plan and purpose; and
A future filled with peace, hope, and prosperity.

(Philippians 4:8) *"Finally, brethren, whatsoever things are true, whatsoever things are honest, whatsoever things are just, whatsoever things are pure, whatsoever things are lovely, whatsoever things are of good report; if there be any virtue, and if there be any praise, think on these things."*

# Section Two (2)

## Words Of Challenge

The poems in Section Two include 1) Steps To Success; 2) Unveiling The Light; 3) Yielded; 4) If, Then; 5) Unity; 6) Love In Action; 7) Godly People; 8) Resurrection.

This section serves to challenge us to a higher standard of accountability, surrender, servant-hood, and love, as individuals and as the corporate body of Christ.

# Steps To Success

Do you know
That the world is an open door
Full of opportunities for you to explore?
For you to make the most of every one,
You will have to work hard
And sacrifice some fun.

To achieve in life,
You must believe in you
And pursue and persevere
To make your dreams come true.
Be willing to be active and participate
And when you schedule an appointment
Don't you dare be late!

In whatever you do, just give your best
And be determined to excel in every single test.
To be successful in society, you'll need a friend,
But only God will see you through until the very end.

If you develop a relationship with God you'll see
That He will guide you to the place
Where you want to be.

God will remove self-doubts and fears
That will hold you back
And help you to replace them
With the skills that you lack.

You must associate with people,
Who are positive,
Who take pride in themselves
And in the way that they live.

Maintain contact with your family
And a church that cares,
For they will love you
And will keep you lifted up in prayer.

(Proverbs 2: 6, 8) *"For the Lord giveth wisdom: out of his mouth cometh knowledge and understanding. He keepeth the paths of the judgement, and preserveth the way of his saints."*

# Unveiling The Light

God, who is the light, has chosen us to belong to Him.
He called us out of darkness and saved our souls,
Which were lost in sin.

God's word is a lamp that lights our path,
He provided it for us to know
That through Christ we have life everlasting
And the power to defeat any foe.

God unfolded His word before us,
Giving understanding to all whom sought.
How much more should we give back to others,
Unveiling the light by which we were taught.

We all should reflect God's glory
As He transforms us to be more like Him.
Shining our inner lights throughout the world,
Eternal lights that should never grow dim.

He commissioned us to go forth teaching,
Making disciples of every nation,
Teaching obedience to His commandments,
Sharing His most precious gift of salvation.

Therefore, let us put on our suit of armor
And lift up the high standard of Jesus Christ.
Let us rejoice and not grow weary
Because we possess the light of life.

(Matthew 28:19-20) *"Go ye therefore, and teach all nations, baptizing them in the name of the Father, and of the Son, and of the Holy Ghost: Teaching them to observe all things whatsoever I have commanded you: and, lo, I am with you always, even unto the end of the world. Amen."*

# Yielded

If you want to be God's servant,
You must first examine self
And be honest and receptive
As He cleans out sinful filth.

God may strip you down to nothing
And chastise you while you're there,
But He'll restore you and remold you
And He'll keep you in His care.

You will find you're more effective
As you strive to be like Him.
It is through God's love and through His grace
That true ministry begins and ends.

If you diligently study the word of God
And invite Jesus on your team,
You will find that you are well equipped
To handle all of Satan's schemes.

(Hebrews 12:11) *"Now no chastening for the present seemeth to be joyous, but grievous: nevertheless afterward it yieldeth the peaceable fruit of righteousness unto them which are exercised thereby."*

# If, Then

If you are blessed with good teaching and preaching
tried and tested to remove all doubt;
If you are taught from the bible, your guideline,
then only its truth you will be about.

If you are slowly digesting the word of God
and applying it to your life;
If God's standards are truly your measure,
then you will not involve yourself in strife.

If you are open and completely yielded
to the Holy Spirit at work within,
Then you will not gossip about others
or tell white lies
because you know they are also sins.

If you are hearing and not doing
and have faith without good deeds,
Then you will never reach the people,
who are hurting and in need.

(James 1:22) *"But be ye doers of the word, and
not hearers only, deceiving your own selves."*

# Unity

United, working together,
That is how we all should be.
Reaching out to help one another,
Building relationships is the key.

If we want to make it through this race
And be victorious unto the end,
Then encourage each other in the faith
And on Jesus completely depend.

Be available in times of a crisis,
Call a brother or sister in need;
Pray for them and pray with them,
Be a blessing and do good deeds.

No more cliques, they separate us;
Let's bridge the gaps that now exist.
Allow God to bond us together,
Loving unconditionally within our midst.


(Psalms 133:1) *"Behold, how good and how pleasant
it is for brethren to dwell together in unity!"*

# Love In Action

They are the spiritual parents of our church;
they have shown their love
and have proved their worth.

Do you love them?

They strive to serve the needs of many;
Who among us ever consider
if they have any?

Do you love them?

In any situation,
their support is always there;
How often do we express interest in them
or show we really care?

Do you love them?

Remember that they are humans,
who also have concerns and needs.
Let's commit to serving them
and make a difference doing simple deeds.

If you love them...

Express your appreciation
with thoughtful deeds of care:
Send a note to say, "You are a blessing"
or call to say, "You're daily in my prayers."

If you love them...

Offer a word of encouragement
or a scripture to brighten their day.

Find out what their interests are,
be a good listener,
give them a chance to say.

If you love them…

Love is more than a feeling
and appreciation is more than a word;
But without action they are merely sentiment
and strictly "for the birds."

Show you love them.

(Galatians 6:6) *"Let him that is taught in the word
communicate unto him that teacheth in all good things."*

# Godly People

Who are godly people?
You may ask yourself today.
Search God's word to find the answer,
Trust His truth to show you the way.

They are people like you and me,
Who once lived a life of sin;
Drawn by the Holy Spirit,
They open their hearts to invite Christ in.

They confess all their sins to Jesus,
Surrendering their wills and selves complete.
They become beautiful new creations,
Laying all their burdens at Jesus' feet.

But that is only the beginning
Because they have not yet arrived;
They will continually reexamine self;
To be more like Christ, they will always strive.

It is a constant inner struggle
To be all that they can be,
To access God's available power,
To live effective, victorious, and free.

They press on in spite of obstacles,
Trusting God to see them through.
They are people of noble character,
Strong, resourceful, and generous too.

They live by God's holy standards
And are obedient to His will;
They yield daily to His Spirit
To maximize their gifts
and develop their skills.

(Philippians 2:12-13) *"Wherefore, my beloved, as ye have always obeyed,
not as in my presence only, but now much more in my absence, work
out your own salvation with fear and trembling. For it is God which
worketh in you both to will and to do of his good pleasure."*

# Resurrection

You can experience the resurrection,
God deemed it so ere time hath begun.
For God so loved the world
That He gave His only begotten Son.

You can experience the resurrection
When you open your heart to Jesus Christ;
You can go through and overcome
The stress, the struggles, and the strife.

You can experience the resurrection
When your past discretions no longer hurt,
and you don't care if the truth comes out
When so called friends try to dish old dirt.

You can experience the resurrection
When you have joy instead of pain,
When you praise God in the midst of battle
Before the victory has been obtained.

You can experience the resurrection,
Growing in the power of Jesus Christ.
You can experience the resurrection
Because He got up after laying down His life!

(Philippians 3:10) *"That I may know him, and the power of his resurrection, and the fellowship of his sufferings, being made conformable unto his death."*

# Section Three (3)

## Words Of Relationship

The poems in Section Three include 1) A Friend; 2) You Are;
3) Special Friend; 4) Hey Love; 5) Our Wedding Day; 6) United;
7) Bittersweet; 8) Family.

This section speaks about relationships of friendship, romance,
marriage and extended family.

# A Friend

A friend is an intimate…
Reaching out to embrace me with love.

A friend is a confidant…
Always listening and encouraging.

A friend is a partner…
Interceding on my behalf in prayer.

A friend is a precious gift…
Packaged by God to reflect His light.

A friend is a blessing…
Inspiring me throughout a lifetime.

A friend is …
YOU

(Proverbs 18:24) *"A man that hath friends must show himself friendly: and there is a friend that sticketh closer than a brother."*

# You Are

You are a friend of mine, a gift from God;
You are an answer to a prayer.
You are a kind, compassionate person,
And a treasure that is truly rare.

You are a sensitive, giving person,
A child of God with a sincere heart.
You earnestly desire to please Him,
Endeavoring to always do your part.

You are an encouraging, thoughtful person;
You have endured and given your best.
You are determined to keep your eyes on Jesus,
Reflecting His spirit through every test.


(Proverbs 17:17) *"A friend loveth at all times,
and a brother is born for adversity."*

# Special Friend

All praises are due to the Father
For His peace and His liberty;
But today, I thank God most of all
For His divinity in you and me.

My friend, you are truly special;
You are loving, giving, and kind.
I enjoy being in your presence
And how you stimulate and challenge my mind.

I love your passion for the people
And your burden for justice and change.
You are a person of strength and character;
You are responsible with priorities well arranged.

Our friendship is progressively evolving,
Our destination, only God can foresee.
I am grateful for our divine relationship;
Indeed, you are a gift from God to me.

(Song of Solomon 2:3) *"As the apple tree among the trees of the wood,
so is my beloved among the sons. I sat down under his shadow with great
delight, and his fruit was sweet to my taste."*

# Hey Love

Hey Love,
Yeah, I'm talking to you … Baby.
You … the gift of love from Love;
I want to saturate you with love.
So, Hey Love this word's for you.

You … with the tender touch that I love so much;
Reached out, reached in
Didn't even see you coming.
Feeling you beyond the physical,
Drawing me magnetically…
Spirit to spirit.

Hey Love,
You … who are oozing intensity,
Anointing me with your passion and sincerity.
Opened me up to pour me out
All over you.

Hey Love,
You … stimulating, got me creating
Must be divine orchestrating.
Can't you feel it too?
You have to know it's true…
Baby, I love you!

(Song of Solomon 5:16) *"His mouth is most sweet; yea, he is altogether lovely. This is my beloved, and this is my friend…"*

# Our Wedding Day

The awaited time has finally come,
For this day we have prepared;
To express our vows to one another
Of the love we will always share.

We will say, "I do" and become as one
In word as well as deed.
And when obstacles come our way in life,
We'll trust God to supply our needs.

We believe in us and shall live by faith,
On God we will depend,
To help us stay joined together,
Forever as lovers,
Helpmeets, and friends.

We extend our love and gratitude
To everyone who has played a part
In making this our most cherished day,
Which has overwhelmed
And blessed our hearts.

(Matthew 19:6) *"Wherefore they are no more twain, but one flesh. What therefore God hath joined together, let not man put asunder."*

# United

Fashioned by the Master's hand
To fit together within His plan;
Me as your woman, you as my man,
To multiply and possess the land.

Made for each other,
Leaving father and mother,
To cleave together and love each other.

Flesh of my flesh,
Bone of my bone,
United as one, creating a home.


(Ephesians 5:31) *"For this cause shall a man leave his father and mother, and shall be joined unto his wife, and they two shall be one flesh."*

# Bittersweet

Bittersweet are the memories that come to my mind
As I ponder our marriage, my dear.
I remember the fights when we nearly broke up,
Then I think of the love that we share.

I perceived you disloyal, became bitter inside
When I was not your priority.
Therefore, up went the walls of defenses within,
So protected from hurt I would be.

Then, the closer I looked at your inner true self,
Your love and sweetness showed through.
I knew in my heart how more deeply I'd hurt
And how void life would be without you.

I reflected on times when sick and in bed,
How tenderly you took care of me.
I realized in order for us to be one,
Removing those walls was the keys.

Time has passed by and our marriage endures,
Through our trials, we have truly been blessed.
I now know both bitter and sweet play a part
To help strengthen our love through each test.

I commit to you now: you are truly my love,
By your side I will forever stand.
With my heart open wide and my love stretching forth,
I give to you all that I am.

(Ephesians 5:33) *"Nevertheless let every one of you in particular so love his wife even as himself; and the wife see that she reverence her husband."*

# Family

What constitutes a family
Is inclusively defined:
It is parents and children, uncle and aunts,
Grands and cousins of yours and mine.

A family is a husband and wife,
It is brothers and sisters too.
Related by blood, or marriage,
Or in Christ Jesus, like me and you.

The family structure has been weakened
Through the distortions of God's plan.
Society has cracked the foundations
With the immoral will of man.

Violence and drugs touch all our lives,
Teen pregnancy and the HIV/AIDS virus too.
Our children are running rampart
And we wonder what to do.

But, God still reigns and is in control,
His word still true and clear.
He will empower us and give direction,
So take heart, we need not fear.

Just follow God's written guidelines
To manage our households well.
Teach our children the Lord's instruction
And do not provoke them to rebel.

Children, honor your fathers and mothers;
Obey your guardians in everything.
God commanded it with a promise
Of long life and your well-being.

Families, be caring in spite of resentments,
Don't hold grudges, forgive all hurts.
Express your love and stay united,
Don't wait till they're six feet under dirt.

(Deuteronomy 7:9) *"Know therefore that the Lord thy God, he is God, the faithful God, which keepeth covenant and mercy with them that love him and keep his commandments to a thousand generations."*

# Section Four (4)

## Words Of Tribute

The poems in Section Four include 1) A Statement Of Love;
2) A Virtuous Woman; 3) The Boss; 4) An Advocate Of Love;
5) A Mother's Tribute; 6) Pastor's Anniversary; 7) Eldership;
8) A Chosen Vessel; 9) An Honor Due; 10) A Woman Of Substance;
11) Parents' Tribute; 12) Educational Praise; 13) New Beginnings;
14) Mixed Emotions; 15) Lasting Bond of Friendship;
16) A New Start.

This section pays tribute to pastors, parents, coworkers, friends,
mentors, and church members, celebrating birthdays, anniversaries,
retirement, new positions, awards, and relocation.

# A Statement Of Love

In honor of you, Pastor,
I give God special praise
Because of your major influence
In how I was spiritually raised.

You taught me the importance of voting
By emphasizing individual responsibility.
I was challenged to finally register;
I learned my vote counted in the community.

You provided opportunities for training
And supplied materials for self-development.
You guided me beyond my limitations
To become bolder and more confident.

I have matured in this life-long journey
Through your ministry and the love you share.
Your preaching has been on target
And your wise counsel is always there.

You are a father, a friend, and a teacher to me;
I am grateful that you've been so dear.
I thank God for His abundant grace and mercy
In blessing you to live through another year.

(Romans 12:10) *"Be kindly affectioned one to another with brotherly love; in honour preferring one another."*

# A Virtuous Woman

You are truly the virtuous woman
Talked about in Proverbs 31.
I love and appreciate you, Mom,
You are blessed in the eyes of your son.

Even now, as I grow through manhood,
Striving to pursue and complete my dreams,
You are there patient and supportive,
You are forever watching over me.

Through my struggles, you have experienced
Just as much if not more pain.
Yet, you listened to my self-pity
And you allowed me to complain.

I celebrate you Mom, Happy Birthday!
You endured and withstood many tests.
I thank you for your love and your guidance;
I thank God for your life, you're the best.

(Proverbs 31:28a) *"Her children arise up,
and call her blessed...."*

# The Boss

Happy Birthday dear Supervisor,
This gift is given to let you know
That I truly appreciate you
For encouraging me to strive and grow.

You are an honorable man, who listens,
And a great boss, who is always fair.
You are a kindhearted, people person,
And a special friend, who is sincere.

I've been inspired through your direction
To take charge and become my best.
Thank you for furthering me in my journey
Along the road leading to success.

(Ephesians 6:7-8) *"With good will doing service,
as to the Lord, and not to men: Knowing that whatsoever good thing any
man doeth, the same shall he receive of the Lord, whether he be bond or
free."*

# An Advocate Of Love

Within our work environment,
Your support was beyond compare.
Through our challenges and our problems,
On our behalf, you were always there.

The employees are very grateful
For a supervisor, who worked with us;
One who listened to the whole story
When our clients complained
And made a fuss.

You are compassionate and persevering,
Indeed, you are mighty in the Lord.
Your selfless giving, even in your struggles,
Bonded our spirits in one accord.

The perceptive way you stood by my side,
Seeing when I was not okay;
And how you ministered to my needs
When I was too overcome to pray.

You reminded me to be thankful
And count my blessings one by one.
You helped me sing praises, recall God's word,
And all the good things that He has done.

Congratulations on your new position,
I know lives will continue to be touched.
God works through you to make a difference;
You are a shining light, who contributes much.

(Romans 12:13) *"Distributing to the*
*necessity of saints; given to hospitality."*

# A Mother's Tribute

I pay tribute to you mother,
On my wedding day;
To let you know I'm still here for you
Although, I am married and have moved away.

You have nurtured and loved me always;
We've been together through thick and thin.
I not only love you for being my mother,
But especially for being my friend.

I thank God for blessing me with you,
A strong support throughout my life.
I will always be your daughter,
Even though I am now a wife.

Rejoice for the good times that we shared
And the times that are yet to come.
Know you are not losing a daughter,
Now you are finally gaining a son.

Be open to God's new direction,
He knows what you are going through.
God does not expect you to be idle,
But to fulfill the work He has called you to do.

Give your talents and time to Jesus,
He will bless you and comfort your heart.
You are needed to further God's kingdom,
Consider this time as a brand new start.

(Proverbs 31:27) *"She looketh well to the ways of
her household, and does eateth not the bread of idleness."*

# Pastor's Anniversary

You are my spiritual father,
My brother and friend in Christ.
You have taught me so much
About God's word
Just by how you live your life.

Your leadership and your guidance,
I would like for you to know,
Have nurtured my spiritual development
And have inspired me to grow.

You have encouraged me through your preaching;
Your prayers have seen me through.
Your wisdom is that of proverbs,
God is doing a mighty work through you.

Your counsel has been enlightening
When I wasn't quite sure what to do.
I've found you to be caring and faithful,
And also steadfast and true.

You are responsible, committed, and tactful;
Your qualities are endless it seems.
You are one who has a vision;
You make reality out of dreams.

I give God thanks for your life;
You have endeared yourself to me.
May God bless you today and forever,
Happy Anniversary!

(Isaiah 11:2) *"And the spirit of the Lord shall rest upon him, the spirit of wisdom and of understanding, the spirit of counsel and might, the spirit of knowledge and of the fear of the Lord."*

# Eldership

Wonderful Elders, worthy of their due,
Studying hard to teach me and you.
Laboring long in word and deed,
Ruling well and meeting people's needs.

Beautiful Elders, standing tall and strong,
Not going along just to get along.
Taking a stand on God's word,
Sowing seeds and interceding to be heard.

Powerful Elders, using healing touch
And the prayer of faith that availeth much.
Anointing with oil, laying on of hands,
Being obedient to what the Lord commands.

Covering Elders, protecting the flock,
Assisting the Pastor,
Buffering some of his hard knocks.
Preparing God's house to edify the saints,
Serving the Eucharist, as often as it takes.

Compassionate Elders, so loving and dear,
Always available to demonstrate they care.
Troubled or sick? Call the Elders for help,
God will raise you up with a story to tell.

(James 5:14-15) *"Is any sick among you? let him call for the elders of the church; and let them pray over him, anointing him with oil in the name of the Lord: And the prayer of faith shall save the sick, and the Lord shall raise him up; and if he have committed sins, they shall be forgiven him."*

# A Chosen Vessel

We chose you as our honoree
To receive this year's award
For your years of faithful service
And your commitment to the Lord.

You are a beautiful, hardworking person,
Always available when called upon.
You demonstrate how to be a team player,
Leaving a legacy for us to build on.

Your perseverance and dedication
Is a witness for all to see;
Your life is truly appreciated
By your church and your family.

(Proverbs 31:31) *"Give her of the fruit of her hands;
and let her own works praise her in the gates."*

# An Honor Due

At our place of worship,
Under your ministry,
I'm both grateful and blessed
That I was led here to be.

Since I've been attending this church,
You've been father and mother,
My counselors, my friends,
And my sister and brother.

You have taught me through God's word
And by the way you live life.
You have discipled and nurtured me
And led me deeper in Christ.

So on this special day
I pay tribute to you
For your kindness, your love,
And the many things that you do.

You are deserving of honor
And encouragement too.
You have served our church well;
Today is your day; it's due!

(Psalms 43:3) *"O send out thy light and thy truth: let them lead me; let them bring me unto thy holy hill, and to thy tabernacles."*

# A Woman Of Substance

To you, a faithful sister
And a woman of quality traits;
You bless our hearts in distinct ways,
This is your life we celebrate.

The youth, adults, and seniors too,
Are touched by your love and care,
By your compassion in times of sorrow,
By your powerful intercessory prayer.

We have been corrected and encouraged
By your candid and truthful talks.
We have grown in our spiritual journeys
Through the example of your Christ-like walk.

We appreciate your joy and willingness
To help others in their time of need.
You go beyond the call of duty;
You get dirty and roll up your sleeves.

You are a dependable warrior of inner-strength,
Firmly committed and genuine.
We thank you for your years of service
As our sister and our friend.

(Proverbs 31:29) *"Many daughters have done
virtuously, but thou excellest them all."*

# Parents' Tribute

A dependable, compassionate woman,
Who is straightforward and inwardly strong;
I remember thinking how strict mom was
For her discipline when I'd done wrong.

I did not appreciate it then,
But since I moved out on my own,
I often think on the things that she said
And taught me when I was home.

My father is a hard working provider
And a caring leader with many things to do;
But, in spite of his busy schedule,
He is always there when I need him too.

I am grateful to my parents
For their consistency and the time
That they have spent in raising me
And keeping me in line.

They sacrificed a lot for me
And labored before the Lord in prayer.
In spite of my mistakes along the way,
They never withdrew their support or care.

(Ephesians 6:2-3) *"Honour thy father and mother; which is the first commandment with promise; that it may be well with thee, and thou mayest live long on the earth."*

# Educational Praise

From the beginning, you sought my best interest
Even though you only received my ungratefulness.
Yet, you still helped me pick up the pieces
When my life fell apart, in a mess.

You stood by me as a surrogate parent,
As my friend and as my advisor too;
Your counsel and the time you invested
Helped me academically and emotionally pull through.

You educated me on a holistic basis;
Your concern, I will forever appreciate.
Your commitment to your students
Truly helped me press forward and graduate.

(Romans 12:11) *"Not slothful in business; fervent in spirit; serving the Lord."*

# New Beginnings

As an employee, you've been consistent;
As a Christian, you've withstood the tests.
As a spouse, you've been supportive;
As a parent, you've done your best.

You deserve congratulations
For reaching to this place,
For being steadfast and diligent,
Which is needed in any race.

You've come this far by the grace of God;
Your faith has seen you through.
And although you are now retiring,
There are new beginnings in store for you.

Look to God for your new directions;
Trust in Him as you've done before.
Be excited and watch with expectancy
As God opens up new doors.

(Isaiah 43:18-19) *"Remember ye not the former things,
neither consider the things of old. Behold, I will do a new thing;
now it shall spring forth; shall ye not know it?
I will even make a way in the wilderness,
and rivers in the desert."*

# Mixed Emotions

Filled with mixed emotions,
You prepared to move away.
Now you have reached the count down
Of your final working days.

It won't be the same without you;
We know some changes will be made
That will cause us to truly miss you
And regret you did not stay.

As an employee and as a person,
You have grown in ways unknown.
Know that God has shown you favor
And wants to love you as His own.

You've experienced extreme stresses
From many hardships, joys, and pain.
But, God's mercy and love endureth;
Throughout your struggles,
You've been sustained.

Remember all of the encouragement
And the comfort you received.
Don't fill the void with imitations,
Turn to God, learn, and believe.

Look to the future with hope and excitement,
Don't be afraid to start anew.
With God as your committed partner,
There is no good thing He will withhold from you.

(Psalms 84:11) *"For the Lord God is a sun and shield;
the Lord will give grace and glory: no good thing will
he withhold from them that walk uprightly."*

# Lasting Bond Of Friendship

I am sincerely going to miss you,
I can sense it in my heart.
True friends are rare and hard to find;
I will be sad when you depart.

But you will never be so far away
That I won't remember you.
You have been a special friend to me,
One who's kind and thoughtful too.

You have touched my life in a unique way,
With your gentleness, wit and style.
We have developed a bond of friendship
That will last despite the distant miles.

I thank God for allowing our paths to cross,
For the friendship, the memories, the fun;
For a relationship that will last a lifetime,
Never to be undone.

(Colossians 3:12) *"Put on therefore, as the elect of God, holy and beloved, bowels of mercies, kindness, humbleness of mind, meekness, longsuffering."*

# A New Start

To our Brother and dear Sister,
We give honor on this special day.
We express our love in tributes,
As you prepare to move away.

At our church, we will surely miss you;
Of yourselves, you have given much.
We have grown from your love and faithfulness,
And our lives have been truly touched.

For ourselves, we are sad you are leaving,
But our hearts are overjoyed too,
Because you've ignited within each other
A love that is fresh and new.

You are never too old for new beginnings,
A new mate, home, and life just for you.
Yes! Everyday is a day of thanksgiving
Because there is nothing that God can't do.

Although you are moving out of town,
You will always have a home with us here.
But, don't be surprised to see many of us
coming over to visit you there.

As you enjoy life in your new residence,
Let's keep one another lifted up in prayer.
Until we see you at the next appointed time,
We'll entrust you into God's care.

(1 Corinthians 2:9) *"But as it is written, Eye hath not seen, nor ear heard, neither have entered into the heart of man, the things which God hath prepared for them that love him."*

# Section Five (5)

## Words Of Comfort

The poems in Section Five include 1) Then And Now, We Honor You; 2) Live On; 3) Honoring The Memory; 4) Follow The Legacy; 5) A Child Of God; 6) Never Alone; 7) Memory Of A Man; 8) The Greatest Worth.

This section is for the encouragement of individuals who experience sorrow from suffering the loss of a loved one, and honors the lives of the deceased.

# Then And Now, We Honor You

Within a ministry spanning 20 years,
Growing in the Power of the Resurrected Christ.
The part you played along the journey, then
Was significant and still influences us, now.
We honor you.

Women available and willing,
Sowing seeds of self-sacrifice.
Sisters, Mothers, Aunties, Nanas…our Godsend, then.
Wise Women, Role Models, Sheroes…our legacy, now.
You were a key factor in "how we got over."
We honor you.

We always knew the time would come,
It's the cycle of this earthly life.
But it came too soon, so much more to be done, then.
Life without you not the same,
Challenged by emptiness and pain, even now.

Yet, we go on with each other
Through Christ who gives us strength.
Until we meet again,
We honor you.

(Hebrews 12:1) *"Wherefore seeing we also are compassed about with so great a cloud of witnesses, let us lay aside every weight, and the sin which doth so easily beset us, and let us run with patience the race that is set before us."*

# Live On

My children, I'll always be with you,
Kept alive through the memories we share.
I will watch over you by both day and night;
Through God's Spirit and love, I'll be there.

Don't attempt to come here with me
Even though you hurt deep in your heart,
Because that is a sin in the eyes of God
And would keep us forever apart.

God has called me home to be with Him,
But you must live to keep my memory alive.
God has a purpose for each of you children
To complete before it's your time to die.

Keep on living, your pain will soon weaken
And the emptiness you feel will pass by.
Be happy for me, I'm in heaven;
God has healed me, no more will I cry.

You can see me in your dreams and photos,
And feel my presence and my love close to you.
Just ask God for His peace and His comfort,
And then trust Him to take you through.

Remember the good that I taught you,
Pass it on, be a blessing in life.
Take one day at a time, God will help you
As you follow the example of Christ.

(Revelations 7:17) *"For the Lamb which is in the midst of the throne
shall feed them, and shall lead them unto living foundations of waters:
and God shall wipe away all tears from their eyes."*

# Honoring The Memory

Although she is gone, she will not be forgotten
If we keep her in our thoughts and in our hearts.
When we reflect upon her life and what she meant to us,
Then her memory will live on and not depart.

If you want to give due honor to her memory,
Then do for others like she always did for you.
Make the best of situations that arise within your life,
Don't quit when things get rough, keep pressing through.

Let this be the start of a new beginning;
Strive to readjust your life to ease the pain.
If you commit to God and allow Him to assist you,
Then the life she lived will not have been in vain.

(II Corinthians 4:16-17) *"For which cause we faint not; but though our outward man perish, yet the inward man is renewed day by day. For our light affliction, which is but for a moment, worketh for us a far more exceeding and eternal weight of glory."*

# Follow The Legacy

She lived a life of faith and prayer,
Endurance, love, and strength.
She never gave up; instead, she persevered
Throughout the trials of her Christian race.

She encouraged people with God's word
And with her testimonies of praise.
She prayed fervently for her family,
For the church, and for God's lost strays.

Her words and deeds expressed her love
And many lives have been touched
By this gentlewoman of deep beauty,
Who has left us with so much.

Her legacy remains with us
In the memory of her life.
She trusted her Jesus and rejoiced
In spite of great personal pain and strife.

She finished the race in victory
And won her just reward.
She has been set free and is now at peace
In her new home with the Lord.

So, shed tears of joy for our sister
And allow God to make you strong.
You will find God's grace sufficient
To carry you along.

If you follow the example of her life,
You will see her again one day.
Just receive God's gift of salvation
And live your life Jesus' way.

(II Thessalonians 2:16-17) *"Now our Lord Jesus Christ himself, and God, even our Father, which hath loved us, and hath given us everlasting consolation and good hope through grace, comfort your hearts and stablish you in every good word and work."*

# A Child Of God

A unique and precious child of God,
Full of love and kindness too.
I remember the times of fellowship
That she enjoyed with me and you.

She helped bond our church together
As we lifted her up in prayer.
We were all united through the love
That Jesus commands for us to share.

I thank God for this dear sister,
Who influenced all our lives.
She was open, honest, full of strength,
And determined to always strive.

We should all be wholly encouraged,
She was faithful unto the end.
She praised God throughout her suffering,
We can be sure she will rise again.

But for now, our dear sweet sister
Is at peace, she fought and won.
She has journeyed home to glory
And is resting in the "Son."

(I Thessalonians 4:16) *"For the Lord himself shall descend from heaven with a shout, with the voice of the archangel, and with the trump of God: and the dead in Christ will rise first."*

# Never Alone

Her suffering is over; she fought a good fight
And has won the reward of eternal life.
She was not forsaken, nor left all alone;
Our God has embraced her and taken her home.

She still remains with us, her spirit lives on.
The memories we share will never be gone.
Her humor, her friendship, her knowledge, her love
Was a blessing to many and a precious gift from above.

She is at rest now, but you can see her again
If you trust in her Jesus as your Savior and friend.

(II Corinthians 1:3-4) *"Blessed be God, even the Father of our Lord Jesus Christ, the Father of mercies, and the God of all comfort; Who comforteth us in all our tribulation, that we may be able to comfort them which are in any trouble, by the comfort wherewith we ourselves are comforted of God."*

# Memory Of A Man

As you dry your eyes,
Look beyond your tears
And remember the jokes
And smiles he shared
With us throughout the years.

His suffering is over
And his pain remains no more,
Remember him through his wife and kids
As the man whom they adored.

See him when you look at them,
Think of times gone by,
Take heart my friends, reminisce with them
And rejoice as well as cry.

Keep his memory alive;
Relive the stories among your friends.
Maintain a positive attitude
And good humor in life till the end.

(II Thessalonians 3:16) *"Now the Lord of peace himself give you peace always by all means. The Lord be with you all."*

# The Greatest Worth

As I ponder on the brevity
of life upon this earth
And consider what one thing
Has proved the greatest worth.

From birth to death,
I think the most important thing to me
Is the relationships we encounter
And how we treat them so casually.

We take our loved ones for granted,
As if they will always be there.
Suffering regrets of "I coulda, woulda, shoulda"
When they are no longer here.

Why can't we heed the wake up calls
Of those who have gone on before?
By showing love and thoughtfulness,
By mending relationships which have been torn.

The past can not be changed
And tomorrow may never come,
Which means today is all we have
To make a difference in the life of someone.

Taking some time for one another,
creatively expressing that we care
Through a phone call, card, or visit
Can lighten the burdens that we bear.

If we stop putting off for tomorrow
What we could do today;
If we follow our inner spirit
When it leads us to have our say.

If we make the most of the time we have
While we are here to do it;
If we take each day as it comes
And live life to the fullest.

Then, maybe when the end draws near
For us and for those we love,
We will know we've done our best
And be at peace for the journey above.

(James 4:14) *"Whereas ye know not what shall be on the morrow. For what is your life? It is even vapour, that appeareth for a little time, and then vanisheth away."*

# Section Six (6)

## Words Of Testimony

The poems in Section Six include 1) The Mountain;
2) How Jesus Sees Me; 3) Life Lessons; 4) My Living Letter Process;
5) Posthumous Love; 6) The Visit; 7) My Maker, My Husband;
8) A Rendering.

This section contains expressions of my personal experiences in Christ
that I pray will serve as a testament of His love and faithfulness to
those who are called according to His purpose.

# The Mountain

I took a trip to the mountain
To draw closer to the Lord.
I took a trip to the mountain
To confront feelings of discord.

I took a trip to the mountain
To see the Holy Spirit manifested in me.
I took a trip to the mountain
To find peace and security.

When I had reached that mountain,
Can you guess what I found there?
On my journey for understanding,
My quest for answers to my prayers.

Through God's omniscient attribute,
He knew all my pressing needs.
God met me on that mountain
Because I yielded to let Him lead.

While I was on that mountain,
God blessed my waking hours.
He revealed to me new insights
Of His love and unlimited power.

I began to feel God's presence
At work inside of me.
And before I left that mountain,
I was at peace in His security.

(Psalms 145:18-19) *"The Lord is nigh unto all them that call upon him, to all them that call upon him in truth. He will fulfill the desire of them that fear him: he also will hear their cry, and will save them."*

# How Jesus Sees Me

Jesus sees me as the Father's daughter,
Whom He died for that I might be saved.
As a much loved, unique, and new creation,
I am fearfully and wonderfully made.

As a confessed and repented sinner,
Forgiven of past, present, and future sins;
As a sacred temple for the Holy Spirit,
I am filled and controlled
By Him who dwells within.

Jesus sees me as one of God's chosen
Set apart for His work to fulfill,
Justified by His grace and His mercy;
I am a disciple doing God's will.

As co-heir with Him in everything,
Inseparable from God's love,
More than a conqueror in all adversities;
I am victorious through Him
Who intercedes above.

Jesus sees me as a patient,
Who needs healing;
As a woman, who endures,
Working through the stress;
As a child, needing hugs of comfort;
I am a witness, who loves God
And holds to His promises.

(I Peter 2:9) *"But ye are a chosen generation, a royal priesthood, a holy nation, a peculiar people; that ye should show forth the praises of him who hath called you out of darkness into his marvellous light."*

# Life Lessons

On my journey, I once chose to do it my way,
even though God tried to tell me what was best.
But, I leaned to my own limited understanding
and rationalized myself into an unfortunate mess.

Fleeing unresolved issues and heart-wrenching
loneliness, I married in spite of Spirit's warning
and fearful doubts.  Although he was a good man,
a minister, and a hard-working provider,
you could be unequally yoked to a Christian
is what I found out.

It took me ten years to confess and repent my disobedience;
emotionally and spiritually, I had slowly begun to die.
The following year, my release came after crying out,
"How long Lord?" For years I thought, "I made my bed,
I have to sleep in it, and stuff the cry."

I am grateful for second chances and new beginnings;
I now know: regardless of what situations I try to create,
God's process for my development and intended purpose
may be delayed or adjusted, but can not be escaped.

I have come full circle to face my fears and trust God;
It was not an option, some things occurred I did not expect.
To achieve my dreams and keep my steps directed,
God orchestrated the removal of all my safety nets.

I walk by faith, stumbling to my divine destination,
desperate to learn from past mistakes and to follow
God's lead.  I can snuggle in God's warm embrace of
unconditional love now, and increase through the
eternal covenant promise, as Abraham's seed.

God, the Father, always desired to give me the kingdom.
He ordained it before I was formed in my mother's womb.
His plans are to prosper me, give me hope, and a future;
not harm me with evil, fear, or irrevocable doom.

I learned to be content, even when I appeared lacking
because long-term finances had yet to become mine.
Through the Word, I attained prosperity of soul and spirit,
realizing the physical manifestation must first begin inside.

I am wealthy with immeasurable bless-ed riches:
I have God's favor, fellowship, power, joy and love.
I have family, friends, a church home, and God's promise
that He will perform the good work in me until Jesus comes.

I don't have to figure out all the details of tomorrow.
I don't have to worry about, "What if I fail or fall?"
I can repent, speak God's word, and trust Him
to fix whatever the situation, great or small.

I am a wonderful creation made in God's image and likeness;
created to love, worship, and give praises to Him;
A chosen vessel and laborer, building up the kingdom.
Without God, I can do nothing;
I need God in order to live.

The Word is eternally relevant for all generations.
Jesus paid the price that holistically sets me free.
Therefore, I rejoice throughout all trials and tribulations;
I am more than a conqueror, the victory is guaranteed!

(Psalms 30:11) *"Thou hast turned for me my mourning into dancing: thou hast put off my sackcloth, and girded me with gladness."*

# My Living Letter Process

My life as a Living Letter
was a prewritten outline before time began,
by my omnipotent, omniscient Creator,
the omnipresent great "I AM".

God called me to repentance
just as I was, there was no need to prepare.
God provided for me the gift of salvation
when I confessed, believed and received
His Love - unconditional and rare.

It's been a "learn as-I-go" process that I often tried
to control while struggling through what I spiritually heard.
Frustrations mounted at times when my growth stagnated
or when my living fell short of God's holy word.

I have learned that: I don't have to know the details,
figuring out how or what to do next. It is God,
who orders my steps and makes my way successful,
orchestrating my world to ensure I am blessed.

I have learned to repent daily, surrendering my will to Jesus;
it is by His power I am transformed and made new.
Under God's anointing, I walk in His favor
radiating His light in everything I do.

I have learned to be satisfied and complete in Jesus
by committing to a daily, quality, quiet time.
I experience intimate, sweet, and loving fellowship
that has strengthened my spirit and developed
a confident, peace-filled mind.

I am learning to trust Jesus and reflect His image
of self-less service throughout my life.
As a Living Letter unfolding to a divine prewritten outline,
I've decided to make godly choices
that victoriously fill in the blanks.

(Psalms 139:16) *"Your eyes saw my unformed body.  All the days ordained
for me were written in your book before one of them came to be."*

# Posthumous Love

It was long after his death, I gave birth to this love.
For most of his life, I was distant and cold.
I only spoke in a manner
that was contemptuous and bold.
I'm not proud, I'm just stating the facts.

We often hear, "Beware the wrath
of a woman scorned";
But the consequences of a brother spurned
can be just as painful, generative, and wrong.

Selfish, irresponsible, and uncaring;
To me, that is where he stood.
I was just too young to remember
the heydays of his fatherhood.

Blinded by partial knowledge and
the stagnant perception of a child;
A hardened heart that would not let me see
the best of him…also present inside of me.

My journey to this posthumous love
began when I got saved.
Forgive to be forgiven was how
this reconciliation road was to be paved.

I grew to speak with a civil tongue
and proactively quench the negative thoughts,
but the desire to demonstrate any love
seemed to be forever lost.

I don't remember ever calling him "daddy"
or saying, "I love you" to his face;
But, I finally got the opportunity to reconcile
thanks to the ministry of Pastor Youngblood
and God's precious grace.

I learned to search out the good and make peace
with his spirit and within myself.
I learned that harboring ill feelings
was self-destructive and that
Love is the key above all else.

I discovered his enriching legacy
transmitted to my sister Renee and me...
his good heart, his sense of humor,
and his dancing ability.

And the one thing that I hold dearest,
my childhood desire, the greatest gift
is my younger brother William; dad's namesake
and physical image, who I met when I was 36.

To conceive this posthumous love
I now experience
for my earthly father, whom gave me life;
I opened my heart and took the steps to grow
in the healing power of the resurrected Christ.

(I Corinthians 13:12) *"For now we see through a glass, darkly; but then face to face: now I know in part; but then shall I know even as also I am known."*

# The Visit

I didn't say, "My heart has ached for your physical presence
for over 20 years."
I didn't see her as a tiny newborn baby in her appearance.
I didn't cry tears of sadness and loss with the thought of her this time.

I said, "I apologize that we didn't have the opportunity
to live our lives together."
I saw her as a 4-year old with a momentary unfamiliar
look in her eyes and hesitancy in her body language.
I hugged her and joyfully tussled with her on the floor
of my meditation created safe place.

I didn't say, "I wish you were alive and able to live with me now."
I didn't see any pain or imperfections in her appearance.
I didn't hold onto the moment as if it were our last.

I said, "I love you and have always loved you."
I saw love, life, and laughter in her spirit and interaction with me.
I released her presence back into the spiritual care of my late grandparents
until our next visit.

(Isaiah 49:13) *"Sing, O heavens; and be joyful, O earth; and break forth into singing, O mountains: for the Lord hath comforted his people, and will have mercy upon his afflicted."*

# My Maker, My Husband

My Maker is my husband;
He has been and will always be.
It took a long while before that knowledge
would satisfy me. Now I accept it
and its value I can plainly see.

I searched many years for external comfort,
Desiring love and companionship in a helpmeet.
Seeing myself divorced, gifted, and filled with potential,
I realized that in God I had already been complete.

I had to examine my inner child and deal with her issues;
She wanted to play and be taken care of.
In her rebelliousness, we acted out of control
Until I surrendered us to unconditional Love.

I asked God, "Why do I entertain non-committal relationships
and yoke myself unequally?"
He said, "You seek to hide to take the edge off of living,
But you need to seek to hide in Me."

He also said, "I Am the Love
you've been seeking, no other person can satisfy.
I receive you unto Me committed
in Love and faithfulness that will never die."

Then He told me, "Prepare your outer being
and I will handle the inner work to be done."
So, I went about making preparations
for my marriage to Jesus Christ, the Son.

On Tuesday, May 1, 2007, during communion service
we became officially engaged.
On May 3, during the National Day of Prayer service
we consummated our spiritual Wedding Day!

Although I still desire an earthly husband,
I am complete, satisfied, and kept by the Lord.
He is preparing me beneath the wings of His protection
Until He releases me unto the man
He deems is in one accord.

(Isaiah 54:5) *"For your Maker is your husband, the Lord Almighty is his name, the Holy One of Israel is your Redeemer; he is called the God of all the earth."*

# A Rendering

What shall I render unto the Lord
For all His benefits towards me?
In the presence of all His people,
I vow a committed life to ministry.

God has graced me with second chances;
He's brought me full circle to face life anew.
His unconditional love heals me, as it nurtures;
I vow trials and transitions I will endure.

I am literally kept by God's provisions;
My faith has deepened; my soul continually lifts.
He stirs my joy and wraps me in His presence;
I vow to embrace and utilize my gifts.

I've learned that one of God's greatest blessings
Is found in the people He lends to our lives;
The s/heroes that inspire by example;
I vow to hold on and to always strive.

What shall I render unto the Lord?
How will I pay my vows?
Through my writings and encouragement of others
To the glory of God, that's how!

(Psalms 116:14) *"I will pay my vows unto the
Lord now in the presence of all his people."*

# Section Seven (7)

## Ethnocentric Expressions

The poems in Section Seven include 1) An Ancestral Encounter; 2) I Apologize…Don't Take This Lightly; 3) Little Girls Lost; 4) Ode To Black Youth; 5) Do You Know? 6) Kujichagulia: Self-Determination; 7) A Black Resurrection; 8) A Prayer of Unity

This section contains expressions of love, support, and expectation of renewal and positive change within the black community, throughout all generations.

The Swahili term MAAFA (pronounced ma-a-fa) is used to define my African people's history of enslavement and suffering. The term was coined by Marimba Ani in her book *Yurugu* and further expounded upon by Erriel D. Roberson in his book *The Maafa & Beyond: Remembrance, Ancestral Connections And Nation Building For The African Global Community.*

# An Ancestral Encounter

African spirits inhabiting dolls.
Healing spirits, healing dolls.
Man spirit, enslaved spirit;
Still spirit, silent spirit.

MAAFA ...A Great Suffering.
The way out is back through!

I give you my ring -- my offering;
To bond, to connect, to bridge...
The chasm of water and blood.

MAAFA ...A Great Calamity.
The way out is back through!

Mind open, heart calling, "Hear spirit, speak spirit."
We walked and lay; I talked and prayed.
"Why can't I hear you?  Why can't I feel you?"

MAAFA ...A Great Disaster.
The way out is back through!

The drawing table is my task;
"What pain do I draw?" my spirit asks.
A man and a woman is what I see,
both possessing God's light individually.
Reaching out toward each other -- torn frustrated and blue.
Separated by a wall of oppression,
seems they can't break through.

Now I must draw my hope on the other side:
I see a man walking tall with pride, approaching
a woman, who's all aglow and smiling wide;
His anticipation passionately mounting with each long stride.

MAAFA ...A Great Tragedy.
The way out is back through!

I leave you placed on holy ground,
not fully connected, still silent, still bound.
I return once again and sit for a while;
prayerfully seeking, I walk down your road a mile.

Connection complete, revelation made clear,
I finally understood why I could not hear, and
why your features were blank, emotions distant and cold,
because back in your day you were tortured and sold.

MAAFA ...A Great Atrocity.
The way out is back through!

To show love to your wife, friends, or family
would expedite your fate as marketable property.
Why feed the oppressors' sickness when he turns the knife.
Why show him your pain while he's destroying your life.

You built up a wall of protection
to mask your spirit from their perverse cruelty.
At the time, it was a tool for your survival;
Generations later, it's a relational issue unfortunately.

MAAFA ...A Great Suffering.
The way out is back through!

As I wept for your yesterdays and our today,
I apologized, vowing that our tomorrows will not stay the same; That I
will help to break the cycle, help to set your spirits free. That I will be
an open vessel, who will dance, sing, write, speak, and love for you. As
a living tribute to my ancestors and a personal blessing to you, honoring
your spirits is what I will do!

MAAFA ...A Great Calamity.
The way out is back through!

Receiving insight into our condition as a people birthed within me a new appreciation for our Black Men and a root understanding of ... absent fathers, stray sons, disrespectful brothers, abusive husbands. Recognizing that while we are sufferers of Post-Traumatic Slavery Disorder, we are also survivors of Willie Lynch conditioning and Institutionalized Foots of Oppression.
We are TEASAFO! (Survivors)

MAAFA ...A Great Disaster.
The way out is back through!

African spirits inhabiting dolls.
Healing spirits, healing dolls.
Man spirit, enslaved spirit;
Holy Spirit, freed spirit!

MAAFA ...A Great Tragedy.
The way out is back through!

(Colossians 1:13-14) *"Who hath delivered us from the power of darkness, and hath translated us into the kingdom of his dear Son: In whom we have redemption through his blood, even the forgiveness of sins."*

# I Apologize...Don't Take This Lightly

To all the Brothers everywhere,
Listen up and lend an ear;
I render this message to all that will hear.
Please be attentive while I share...and
Don't take this lightly.

To all the Brothers who suffer stress, rejection and pain
when the love you give to Sisters seems to be in vain.
To all the Brothers being arrested due to vindictive games,
I APOLOGIZE.

To all the Fathers whose children are used as pawns
to set you up by being born or withheld from you
when their mothers feel scorned, I APOLOGIZE.

To all the Sons beat down from verbal abuse
By misplaced angers for fathers you didn't choose;
For all the people who think you have no good use,
I APOLOGIZE ...Don't take this lightly.

To our Sons coming up, you are our future and hope.
Stop trying to be down, resist gang banging,
and flee from dope.
Discover who you are and find constructive ways to cope.
Don't take this lightly.

Sons, you have opportunities to reach the highest heights.
Fathers, you can make amends for being out of sight.
Brothers, who have made mistakes, it's not too late to live life right.
Don't take this lightly.

I thank you for your presence; it is regal and strong.
You are a covering for us Sisters, by our side you belong.
Our destiny, slavery tried to squelch but only served to prolong.
Don't take this lightly.

Stay around
Stand your ground
You will abound
Victory!

Don't take this lightly.

(I Corinthians 12:26) *"And whether one member suffer, all the members suffer with it; or one member be honoured, all members rejoice with it."*

# Little Girls Lost

Faces drenched in secret tears,
Gut wrenching pain from inner wounds;
Nubian babies birthing babies
Way too soon.

Abused parents, never nurtured,
Passed down legacies of doom.
Little girls lost with thirsting hearts,
Desperate to fill deserted rooms.

Can you hear the silent screams
Echoing through the dismal night?
Can you see the fear attacking?
In the mind, begins the fight.

Can you feel the numbness growing?
Protective walls standing upright.
Can you taste the bitter fragrance?
Little girls lost, pungent with spite.

She ponders the question of:
What can effectively be done
For little girls lost to experience victory,
Live safe, and have some fun?

The answer: Accept the Lord, Christ Jesus
As your Savior and God's Son.
He will provide your every need
And become your trusted companion.

He will restore you and transform you,
Make you radiant and new.
You will blossom in His love,
Learn to receive, and give love too.

He will prepare you and equip you
With a plan for you to do.
Little girls lost, born with a purpose
Divinely designed for a unique you.

(II Corinthians 5:17) *"Therefore if any man be in Christ, he is a new creature: old things are passed away; behold, all things are become new."*

# Ode To Black Youth

You are somebody...
Wonderfully created by the Lord.

You are somebody...
Striving to live in one accord.

You are somebody...
Filled with unlimited potential.

You are somebody...
Young, Black, Proud, Unique and Special.

You can make a difference...
Valuing your education and history.

You can make a difference...
Demonstrating God's love and unity.

You can make a difference...
Following the guidelines of Jesus Christ.

You can make a difference...
Committing to be examples with your lives.

You will succeed...
In spite of oppression and personal strife.

You will succeed...
Persevering to overcome all obstacles in life.

You will succeed...
Regardless of sex, height, weight, complexion or society's labels.

You will succeed...
Because you are determined, resilient, and able.

(Philippians 1:6) *"Being confident of this very thing, that he which hath begun a good work in you will perform it until the day of Jesus Christ."*

# Do You Know?

Do you realize who you were
Before the MAAFA experience?
Or how you endured and persevered
Through slavery and reconstructed racism?

Do you understand the real story
And not just the white-washed history?
It must be learned and taught to our children,
So that they too can pass on our rich legacy.

Do you know you were destined for greatness
And that you were created to be kings?
You can be leaders of this nation,
Yes, through Christ you can do all things.

Do not be deceived by the dominant culture,
You are brilliant, beautiful, and bold.
The only thing that is truly endangered
Are the historical lies that we've been told.

Strength and healing can be found in each other,
Trust God to direct and provide the tools.
Become like iron sharpening iron,
Cut deep to the core when they change the rules.

We are your sisters, daughters, wives, and mothers,
Standing beside you in respect, support and prayer.
As you reclaim your place of leadership,
Know that you are loved and the burden is shared.

(Proverbs 27:17) *"Iron sharpeneth iron; so a man sharpeneth the
countenance of his friend."*

# Kujichagulia: Self-Determination

Snatched from the Motherland,
demeaned and stripped of our regal essence.
Enslaved, assimilated, and systematically
kept under oppressions feet.
It's time to re-define ourselves and reclaim
our Royal Black Heritage: We are a chosen,
beautiful people and it's our time to reap!

In defining ourselves, we reject media's negative portrayals,
and affirm our brilliant ancestry resilience spread across this land.
It's our responsibility to boldly declare our substance;
It's time to reflect and determine a personal statement to
"Who I Am."

"What's in a name?" is a question to be pondered
when we are naming ourselves, our friends, and our families.
Consider the meaning and the distinctive traits we want to live up to;
choose names that represent quality,
instead of something disparaging.

We are gifted people, divinely blessed with skills and talents.
We possess the power to be creatively self-employed.
We can create various jobs for ourselves and for other Black people.
We must embrace this truth and support our daring entrepreneurs.

In speaking for ourselves, we diversely demonstrate our valor: Teaching
the truth of our life experiences and our Black History.  Conveying
through our music, our voices, our written word, our dancing...
How we survived slavery and endure oppression with bravery.

When we unite and practice principles like those of Kwanzaa,
becoming responsible for and within our communities, we can each
make a difference in our own lives and in the lives of others;
There'll be no stopping us now, we'll be living in victory!

(I Timothy 5:1-2) *"Rebuke not an elder, but entreat him as a father; and
the younger men as brethren; The elder women as mothers; the younger as
sisters, with all purity."*

# A Black Resurrection

A new day dawned, on October 16th,
for the Black Man, when you rose up
to unite with your brothers and take a stand.
You sought oneness with God, atonement
to family and community, self-determination
to be the head and implement demands.

The Million-Man March was a tremendous success
for you dear brothers, an ocean of Black Men,
peaceful and loving, impressive to see.
What an awesome presence you made
on that day, over in Washington,
A ray of hope for our people and a victory.

The Black Woman supported you
with our love and encouragement;
We prayed you through, took care of home,
and felt great pride.
We are thankful for your timely resurrection
to fulfill your destiny in this world
with us, side by side.

We overcame barriers of religious affiliations,
  civil, fraternal, and political ones as well.
We saw the economic advantage
of pooling our own resources
to buy, to set up, to manufacture,
to market, and to sell.

Where do we go from here
my Brothers and Sisters?
For there is no turning back,
we must maintain a new legacy:

Standing together at last,
a progressive, responsible people:
The Black Man, the Black Woman,
and the Black Family.

(Romans 15:5-6) *"Now the God of patience and consolation grant you to be likeminded one toward another according to Christ Jesus: That ye may with one mind and one mouth glorify God, even the Father of our Lord Jesus Christ."*

# Prayer Of Unity

Hear O Lord this prayer
I offer in this consecrated place:
May you impart a spirit of unity
To inhabit the people of our Black race.

May you allow us to experience
How wonderful and pleasant it can be
For Black people to live together
In bless-ed harmony.

Clothe us in unconditional love,
Which bonds all things perfectly,
Open our ears that we may hear
And our eyes that we may see.

Help us to better understand ourselves
And the part that we each should play,
So that we not only hear your word,
But be doers of what you say.

It is written
that what we bind and loose on earth
Will be bound and loosed in heaven:
We loose the spirit of unity
And bind internalized oppression.
We bind the spirit of division,
Low self-esteem, racism, and fear.
We loose race-pride, confidence, self-love,
And a communal spirit of care.

Teach us to reclaim what was stolen
During the MAAFA and slavery.
Heal us from the post trauma
That we may persevere to victory.

Break the perpetual cycle of curses,
Which permeates each generation.
Bridge the relational gaps among our people
In every type of situation.

Show us what we each should do
And how to use what we have, where we are.
Let us not become weary and give up,
For in due season we will reap a reward.

Guide us through our strength in Christ
To do the all that we can.
Convict us to obey your word
For forgiveness and a healed land.

Plant your love in the soil of our hearts
And tenderize us to be good ground.
Let it take root and transform us
To make a difference where any need is found.

Now Father, it is also written that
If two of us agree
About anything that we ask for,
It will be done in heaven by Thee.

So we come to you with confidence
In accordance to your will,
Knowing that you hear us Lord
And our petitions you will fulfill.

We thank You now for positive change
And the authority to rebuke all strife.
By faith, we believe You for Black Unity
In the name of our great high priest
Jesus Christ.  Amen.

(Isaiah 61:7-8) *"Your shame and disgrace are ended.  You will live in your own land, and your wealth will be doubled, your joy will last forever.  The Lord says: 'I love justice and I hate oppression and crime.  I will faithfully reward my people and make an eternal covenant with them.'"*

# About The Author

Jo Anne Meekins has worked as a Procedure Writer for one of New York City's leading health care plans since 2003. She is also a member of the National Writers Union and the Fellowship of Christian Poets, and currently resides in the Bronx, NY.

Jo Anne's talent for writing poetry was first revealed in Junior High School 231, where she discovered her ability to write poetic narratives about her friends. After a long season of an emotional writing block, Jo Anne's gift was prayerfully resurrected while attending New York Institute of Technology, where she earned a Bachelor of Science degree in Community Mental Health (1983).

Her creativity flourished as a new Christian in her first church, where she was requested to write and read poems for various events throughout her membership. Encouraged by the recognition of her gift, Jo Anne obtained a certificate in Basic Journalism and Poetry from the Writers Institute (1993).

Supported by her church and armed with a certificate from the "Be Your Own Boss Entrepreneurship Program," Jo Anne started a home-based business (Express Yourself Creations, 1993) that provided Desktop Publishing Services and specialized in framed Personalized Poetry. To enhance her skills and increase marketability, Jo Anne later received certificates in Communication Skills from the NYU School of Continuing and Professional Studies (2002), and Computerized Office Technology from the Queens Adult Learning Center (2003).

Spanning a period from 1990 through the present, Jo Anne has had articles, poems and announcements printed in the following publications and websites:
Magazines - The Shining Light, Vital Christianity, and Punctuations; Newsletters - SHARE, Between The Lines, The Triple E, and Intercession; Newspapers - The WAVE and The New York Christian Times; Poetry Anthology - A Time To Be Free, Vol. XII (Quill Books); and Websites - www.crossroadstabernacle.com and www.christianpoets.com.

Gifted To: _____

From: _____

Occasion: _____

Date: _____

**\*\*\*\*\*\*\*\*\*\*\*\*\*\*\*\*\*\*\*\*\*\*\*\*\*\*\*\*\*\*\*\*\*\*\*\*\*\*\*\*\*\*\*\*\*\*\*\*\*\*\*\*\*\*\*\*\*\*\*\***

Beloved _____,
　　　　　(Write Your Name Here)

Be encouraged and may God's choicest blessings
abound in your life from this day forth.
In Jesus' name, amen.

*Jo Anne Meekins*

Thank you for purchasing <u>On Solid Ground: Inspirational Poetry for All Occasions</u>. Any and all comments about the book are welcomed and appreciated. Please send to: eycjm@aol.com

Printed in the United States
202110BV00004B/46-66/P